FACES · OF
BRITISH
THEATRE

Gemma Levine

INTRODUCTION BY JONATHAN MILLER

PREFACE BY SIR JOHN GIELGUD

FACES · OF BRITISH THEATRE

PHOTOGRAPHY GEMMA LEVINE

Gemma Levine

PRION

ACKNOWLEDGEMENTS

I would like to express my personal thanks and gratitude to
Chris of Gordon Bishop Laboratories, for the printing of the negatives;
Ghita Cohen and Associates at the Royal National Theatre;
Adrian Gray, who designed this book, for his impeccable
care and creative layout of the photographs;
Hasselblad, the camera I cannot do without;
Ilford Photo UK, who supplied the film;
Olav Wyper, my manager, for his continuous support.

First published in the United Kingdom 1990 by
PRION, an imprint of Multimedia Books Limited,
32–34 Gordon House Road, London NW5 1LP

Photographs copyright © Gemma Levine 1990
Text copyright © Michael Codron, Dame Judi Dench,
Sir John Gielgud, Jonathan Miller, John Mortimer, Carl Toms
Compilation copyright © Multimedia Books Limited 1990

Editor: Anne Cope
Designer: Adrian Gray
Production: Arnon Orbach and Hugh Allan

British Library Cataloguing in Publication Data
Gemma, Levine
    Faces of British theatre
    1. Great Britain. Theatre. Actors & actresses
    I. Title
    792.0280922

    ISBN 1–85375–097–2

Typesetting by Wyvern Typesetting Limited, Bristol, England
Printed in Hong Kong by Imago

For my dear friend,
who has given love and encouragement

I feel privileged to have met some of the most eminent
exponents of British theatre today, even though my
encounters with them have been transitory. Many more faces
of theatre were invited to be included, but for various
reasons could not participate.
As the slave said to Cleopatra, I am only a messenger
and I am only passing on to you. . .
Faces of British Theatre.

GEMMA LEVINE

SIR JOHN GIELGUD

Sir John Gielgud, possessor of the finest speaking voice in the English language, has played almost all of Shakespeare's heroes and directed many sparkling productions (*The Importance Of Being Earnest* at the Globe and Phoenix, *Lady Windermere's Fan* at the Haymarket, *Much Ado About Nothing* at Stratford, *Hamlet* on Broadway, *The Constant Wife* at the Albery). His solo Shakespeare, *The Ages Of Man*, has been acclaimed by audiences worldwide. His career is, *in parvo*, a history of the 20th-century British theatre.

PREFACE BY SIR JOHN GIELGUD

In sitting many hundreds of times for my photograph over the sixty years of my long career, as well as for a considerable number of portraits and sculpture, I have always been fascinated by the complicated relationship between the artist and his model. When the sitter is also an actor, there is bound to be a further difficulty to be resolved, for he has long been accustomed to present his personality in many different guises, both on and off the stage. Now, however reluctantly, he must reveal his private image to the concentrated gaze of someone whom he has met only briefly, a complete stranger who has had to sum him up in a very short time and who is also concerned at the same sitting with the professional details – lighting, posing, focusing, and so on – which must necessarily occupy a photographer's attention.

Painters and sculptors are able to confirm their first impressions in a series of consecutive sittings, but the photographer has only one short session in which to establish the necessary rapport with his subject. Gemma Levine seems able, in my case at any rate, to create an immediately friendly and perceptive attitude, which helped me to relax under her steadfast gaze, and to release some of my inhibitions, caused by a mixture of natural vanity and intrinsic shyness.

It is an unexpected pleasure to submit oneself to an artist whom one can relax with on such easy terms and whose pictures are so successfully expressive. The indefatigable attentions of press photographers, paparazzi and stage-door fans – the last of whom have now become ruthlessly addicted to a demand for snapshots as well as autographs when one is tired after a performance – these added perils to one's privacy must necessarily be considered as part of an actor's professional exposure. But to be photographed by an artist of Gemma Levine's quality and expertise is a delightful change, and her work in this book bears ample witness to her memorable achievements.

John Gielgud.

JONATHAN MILLER

Jonathan Miller is an accomplished director and presenter of theatre, opera, film and television. He directed Olivier in *The Merchant Of Venice* at the National Theatre in 1970, *Rigoletto* and *The Mikado* for ENO in 1982 and 1986, and *Long Day's Journey Into Night* on Broadway and at the Haymarket in 1982. Since 1988 he has mounted an ambitious programme at the Old Vic (*The Tempest, Candide, King Lear, The Liar*).

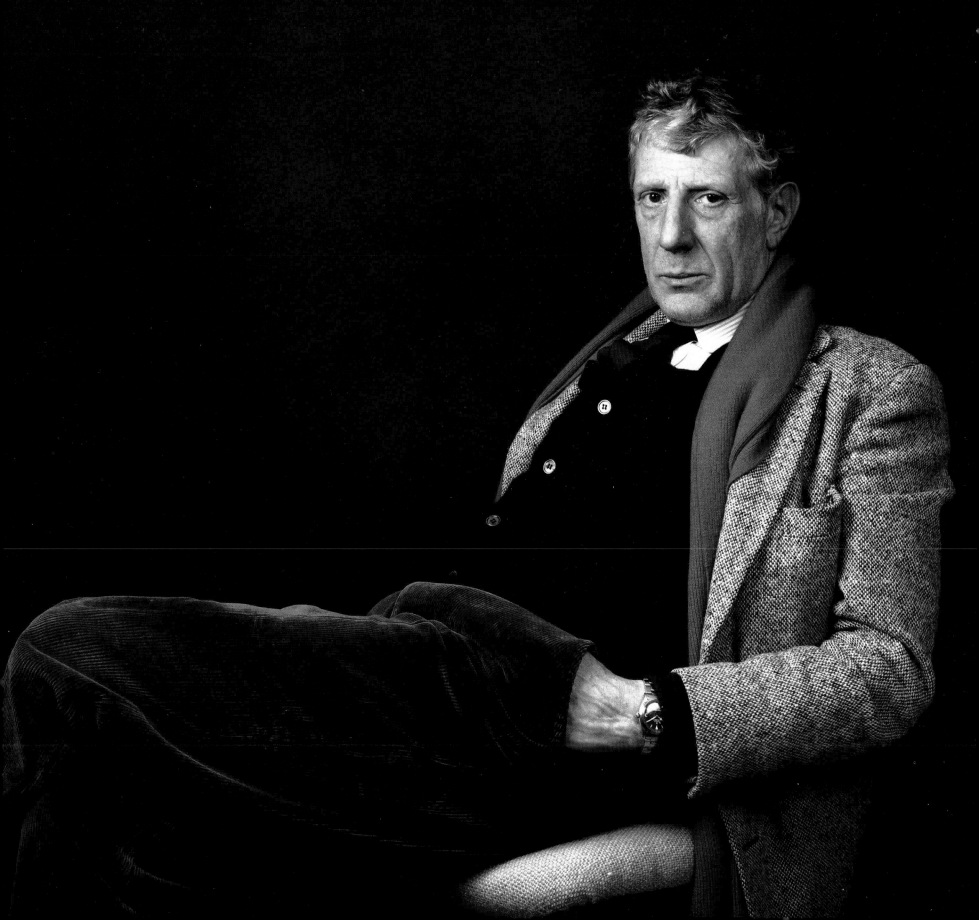

INTRODUCTION BY JONATHAN MILLER

What a difficult task it must be to compile a representative album of the British Theatre! Gemma Levine's admirable collection of photographs is more comprehensive than most, and yet the profession is so large and so enviably accomplished that the list of people who deserve to be included is longer than any purchasable volume can contain. The result is an invidious process of selection and the survivors are not necessarily the fittest. Or to put it more charitably, for any one artist who gets into the book there are three or four others who should have been included. At a conservative estimate there must be at least two hundred artists whose distinguished work is collectively responsible for the almost mythical reputation of the British Theatre. That means designers and directors as well as actors.

Some of the people I have in mind are referred to as actors' actors, which is another way of saying that although they don't necessarily get into collections like this and they're not always to be seen grasping the trophies handed out at award ceremonies, many of them would figure prominently in any poll canvassed within the profession. Because, contrary to popular belief, actors are quick to recognise the distinctive talents of their own colleagues and often complain that work which they discriminatingly admire is overlooked or damned with ignorantly faint praise.

One problem is that the theatre is divided into four estates and although there is fairly free traffic between them all, unless an artist has been conspicuously represented either in the West End or in one of the great national com-

Group Théâtre Complicité, founded in 1983 by Simon McBurney, Marcello Magni and Annabel Arden.

panies, it's difficult to establish the sort of name which publishers find attractive. And yet, as everyone in the profession knows, distinguished work is consistently done both in the provinces and, of course, on the London Fringe – that is to say, in small theatres like The Bush, The Gate, Soho Poly, etc., etc. Admittedly the hierarchy of prestige is not as steep as it is in the United States, where Broadway in all its vulgar triviality is still unaccountably regarded as the peak of an artist's achievement and regional theatre is visualised as a cultural Siberia rarely, if ever, visited by the main New York critics. In Britain, partly because of its small size, the distinction between metropolitan and provincial theatre is less clear-cut. So that productions in Bristol, say, or in Nottingham, Leicester and Glasgow, are frequently reported in the national press. But even so, the magnetic power of the centre is much stronger than it should be and the reputation, or at least the charisma, of an artist still depends unduly on his or her metropolitan visibility. And in the same way, although much more serious attention is given to the London Fringe than the New York critics give to off, and now off-off, Broadway, there is still the irresistible suspicion that any director, designer or actor who is applauded for work done in a pub or warehouse needs to be 'taken up' by the RSC or the National before he or she can claim success.

The only other way in which a performer can 'break through' or anyway give and have the impression that he or she has broken through, is by appearing conspicuously on television. By winning broad popularity on the box, especially in one of the long-running soaps or sitcoms, an actor can earn a name which might otherwise have taken years of unrecognised and poorly rewarded work in the live theatre. In fact, there is no equivalent to the sort of fame and glamour which can be achieved by appearing on television. Understandably this has had a regrettable influence on the theatre, particularly in the West End where commercial managements are increasingly tempted to build productions around well-known 'personalities'. One of the reasons is that inflation has prohibitively increased costs of all but the most modest productions and since West End managements do not have the advantage of a national subsidy the only way of protecting their backers' investment is to guarantee a large advance with the promise of a well-known name. This does not mean that a performer who has won fame on the box is a dud by definition, or that anyone who gets star billing on Shaftesbury Avenue should have paid his or her dues in exclusively live performances. On the contrary, television has an uncanny way of spotting and developing talents which might have gone unnoticed in the conventional theatre. And anyway, the peculiarity of the medium itself means that TV is responsible for creating altogether new idioms of performance, especially naturalistic ones.

Still, the fact remains that, being a mass medium, television unarguably breeds a morbid form of celebrity, not only for the person who enjoys it individually, but more generally by creating a climate of opinion in which public visibility is regarded as a criterion of artistic worth and where chronic invisibility is all too often seen as a sort of stigma. Although the commercial theatre is particularly susceptible to this influence, the subsidised companies are not as chastely immune as they would like us to believe.

In any case, the great national companies are implicated in yet another distortion. By advertising, or at least by not denying the claim, that they are centres of excellence, the National and the RSC help to create the belief that an artist who works under either of these two banners has somehow 'made it' and that the other theatres are no more than testbeds and wind tunnels for models which have still to prove their worth. Whereas the fact is that although memorable productions appear, and will continue to appear, in both of the big subsidised theatres, neither of these establishments can realistically claim that they have a monopoly of excellence or that they set the standards to which all other institutions should pluckily aspire. Apart from the fact that it is a vulgar, copywriters' notion, the idea of excellence is extremely indeterminate, and far from being exemplified in certain centres specially set aside for the purpose, it is often the peripheral theatres which redefine the meaning of the term. For example, under the inspired direction of Giles Havergal, Philip Prowse and Robert David Macdonald, the Glasow Citizens' Theatre, working with a small fraction of the National's budget, has pioneered a genuinely European style of production. Meanwhile, on the Fringe, the Théâtre de Complicité has set an unprecedented standard of idiosyncratic energy and imagination. Cheek By Jowl is yet another force to be reckoned with. In fact, if one surveys the British theatrical scene overall, the idea that excellence is centred in any way seems altogether laughable. Perhaps it's wishful thinking on my part, but I suspect that the theatre is about to undergo a rejuvenating fragmentation and that the already out-dated concept of generously endowed metropolitan flagships will seem absurd in a few years' time.

Conceived and built before inflation set in, these expensive institutions are now overstretched and most them are seriously 'in the red'. The recent shutdown at the Barbican is symptomatic of the crisis. But even if funds were available – and I suspect that a less monetarist government would find it quite as hard to justify forking them out – the output of these theatres is so large that it defeats the promise of consistent excellence. There is also the argument that with two large companies, each of which has to fill at least two auditoria, London is extravagantly over-supplied with 'serious' theatre. There may be too many productions chasing what looks like a diminishing audience.

Of course it's hard to say exactly how many people are going to the theatre at any given time and it could be that if one makes an allowance for the huge bookings for West End musicals the aggregate audience is just as large as ever. But that could be the problem. If, as many professionals suspect, public taste is increasingly biased in favour of exotic light entertainment, the audience for so-called serious theatre is no longer big enough to go round, or not enough to fill several sizeable auditoria, week after week. Whereas it's relatively easy to pack a small house, where the productions are less expensive to mount in the first place. That perhaps is one explanation for the success of companies such as Cheek By Jowl, the Young Vic and, more recently, the Almeida. Another reason is the conviviality of small spaces and the intensity of plays performed with great simplicity. Audiences seem to enjoy this almost congregationalist set-up and actors are often much happier in these circumstances. Apart from the fact that their performances get a more favourable showing when the production isn't overwhelmed by 'imaginative' scenery, the working conditions are much friendlier than

Giles Havergal, Philip Prowse and Robert David Macdonald of the Citizens' Theatre, Glasgow.

they are in the large, somewhat impersonal companies. And although the pay is much less and the prestige arguably smaller, more and more actors are prepared to sacrifice both in the belief that it is a more satisfying way of displaying their craft.

One way or another the British theatre is in a state of flux and it is hard to predict how things will settle down as we enter the last years of the twentieth century. To paraphrase Philip Larkin, theatre of some sort will go on, and even if large, often vulgar, entertainments flourish, 'someone will forever be surprising a hunger in himself to be more serious, gravitating with it' to this or that space, recognising that, at its best, theatre is somewhere 'to grow wise in'.   JONATHAN MILLER

BEN KINGSLEY

Ben Kingsley proved himself at the RSC in *Nicholas Nickleby*, *Othello* and *The Merry Wives Of Windsor*, and at the National in *Volpone* and *The Cherry Orchard*, before winning an Oscar and international fame for his portrayal of Gandhi in Richard Attenborough's film.

SARAH BRIGHTMAN

Sarah Brightman, formerly of Pan's People and Hot Gossip, met her future husband, Andrew Lloyd Webber, while successfully auditioning for *Cats*. *Phantom Of The Opera* was created especially for her.

MAUREEN LIPMAN &
JACK ROSENTHAL

Maureen Lipman began her theatrical career at the National
Theatre, then made her name in TV and in stage comedies such
as *Outside Edge, See How They Run* and *Wonderful Town*. Her
one-woman show as Joyce Grenfell in *Re. Joyce* was a triumph.
She is seen here with her husband, Jack Rosenthal, author
of several stage plays, including *Dear Anyone*, and of more
than 250 plays for television, including *Bar Mitzvah Boy*
and *London's Burning*. With Barbra Streisand he wrote
the screenplay for *Yentl*.

BRIAN COX

Brian Cox began his career in Edinburgh at the Lyceum. In London, his most impressive roles have been Danton in *Danton's Death* and Brutus (both at the National), Titus Andronicus and Petruchio at the RSC, and the tough RUC cop in *Rat In The Skull*, which he also played on Broadway.

SALLY DEXTER

Sally Dexter played Lady Macbeth for the National Youth
Theatre and various roles at the Nottingham Playhouse, then
became a National Theatre player, appearing in Sir Peter
Hall's *The Tempest* and *All's Well That Ends Well*. In 1989
she played Titania in *A Midsummer Night's Dream* and
Viola in *Twelfth Night* in Regent's Park.

RICHARD HUDSON

Richard Hudson's designs were an essential element in the success of *Andromache*, *Too Clever By Half* and *Candide* during the 1988 Old Vic season. His opera designs have included *Count Ory* and *A Night At The Chinese Opera* for Kent Opera, *Manon* for Opera North, and *La Vie Parisienne* for Scottish Opera.

DAME PEGGY ASHCROFT

Dame Peggy Ashcroft has played most of Shakespeare's heroines since playing Desdemona to Paul Robeson's Othello in 1930. Among a multitude of classical roles, she is especially remembered for her Ibsen heroines. She has also appeared at the National (*Happy Days, Watch On The Rhine*) and at the RSC (*All's Well That Ends Well*).

NIGEL HAVERS

Nigel Havers has used his aristocratic looks to great effect on stage in *Conduct Unbecoming, The Importance Of Being Earnest* (National, 1982) and *Other Places* (part of a Pinter triple bill at the National in 1982). Many film and TV engagements followed his performance in *Chariots Of Fire*.

JULIET STEPHENSON

Juliet Stephenson made her mark at the RSC as Rosalind,
Cressida, Isabella, Titania, and Madame De Tourval in
Les Liaisons Dangereuses. Her Yerma and Hedda Gabler at the
National have placed her securely in the top rank.

PAUL SCOFIELD

Paul Scofield's greatest asset is his remarkably flexible voice, used to marvellous effect in plays such as *A Man For All Seasons*, *The Government Inspector*, *The Tempest*, *King Lear*, *Savages*, *Othello*, and *Amadeus*, in which he created the role of Salieri.

IAN MCKELLEN

Ian McKellen established his reputation as a leading
classical actor in 1969–70 in the roles of Richard II and
Edward II for the Prospect Touring Theatre. Macbeth, Hamlet
and Coriolanus followed, to great acclaim. He has also
starred in modern plays such as *Bent* (1979 and 1990),
Wild Honey (1986) and *Henceforward* (1988).

SINEAD CUSACK & JEREMY IRONS

Sinead Cusack, one of the three actress daughters of Irish actor
Cyril Cusack (they all appeared together in *The Three Sisters* in 1990),
was with the RSC for 10 years, playing Beatrice, Portia and
Lady Macbeth. She is pictured here with her husband, Jeremy Irons,
who began his stage career at the Bristol Old Vic. He has appeared in
The Real Thing on Broadway and also as Richard II at the RSC.
His 1986–87 RSC season also included *The Winter's Tale*, *The Rover*
and *Wild Oats*.

ALAN BATES

Alan Bates' prestigious stage and film career began in 1956 when he played Cliff in John Osborne's *Look Back In Anger*. The parts he created in plays by Harold Pinter and Simon Grey were special landmarks. He is also a fine Shakespearean actor. Most recently he has appeared in Shaffer's *Yonadab* at the National, *A Patriot For Me* and *Melon* at the Haymarket, and *Much Ado About Nothing* and *Ivanov* at the Strand.

GERALDINE JAMES

Geraldine James's stage credits include *The Passion Of Dracula* at the Queens, *When I Was A Girl I Used To Scream And Shout* at the Whitehall, and *Cymbeline* at the National. Her recent performance as Portia to Dustin Hoffman's Shylock in London and on Broadway was much praised.

MICHAEL GAMBON

Michael Gambon, is one of the most sought-after leads in British theatre today. His reputation grew in *Galileo*, *King Lear* and *View From The Bridge* at the National, and in plays by Alan Ayckbourn (*The Norman Conquests*, *Just Between Ourseleves*, *A Chorus Of Disapproval*, *A Small Family Business*, *Man Of The Moment*).

FELICITY KENDAL

Felicity Kendal spent her childhood touring India with her
parents' theatre company. In England, she gained fame in
The Norman Conquests, Clouds, Othello, Amadeus and
The Real Thing. She has recently starred with Alan Bates in
Ivanov and *Much Ado About Nothing* at the Strand.

ANTHONY HOPKINS

Anthony Hopkins built a following in the United States in
the 1970s, then returned to the English stage to give
powerful performances as Mark Anthony and King Lear at the
National, as the ruthless newspaper tycoon in *Pravda*, also
at the National, and in the hugely successful *M. Butterfly*.

SIR ANTHONY QUAYLE

Sir Anthony Quayle (1913–1989), who ran the Shakespeare
Memorial Theatre from 1949 to 1965, fulfilled a
long-standing ambition when he formed his own company, the
Compass Theatre Company, in 1983. Of all his stage and
screen roles, Falstaff was his favorite.

MICHAEL CODRON

Michael Codron has produced many successes by Alan Ayckbourn, Alan Bennett, Michael Frayn and Tom Stoppard. As a young producer he took risks on unknown writers such as Harold Pinter, Joe Orton and Christopher Hampton.

What do *producers* look like? The famous actors that grace this book will, to the ordinary reader, immediately strike him as having features which mark them out for fame in their chosen vocation. The other creative artistes featured here have a certain something which stamps them as gifted. But producers? Aren't they more like other businessmen? For essentially that is what they have to be to stay alive as producers, impresarios or theatrical entrepreneurs. And like all businessmen their preoccupations will be with the raising of capital to launch a new project, seeing that money is properly spent and that costs are kept within budget; watching too that the returns remain healthy, for indeed therein lies, for a producer, the real romance of the theatre.

So producers don't really look like anything in particular. I hope that we can convey a liking for our profession and a concern for those we work amongst, because the going at times is so tough, unpredictable, and let's face it, heartbreaking – as it is of course for actors, writers, etc., etc., etc. – that to lose the initial passion for the theatre would make everything else meaningless. So optimism has to be the order of the day. Perhaps that's what producers look like – optimists.

MICHAEL CODRON

DI TREVIS

Di Trevis, who began her career as an actress at the Glasgow Citizens', became the first woman director to be given her own company at the National. Her productions have included Brecht's *The Mother, School For Wives, Much Ado About Nothing* and *Yerma*.

PRUNELLA SCALES &
TIMOTHY WEST

Prunella Scales has played classical roles, appeared in West
End comedies, and starred in many TV sitcoms. Her range is
remarkable. Her recent roles have included Queen Elizabeth II
in Alan Bennett's *Single Spies* and Mrs Candour in
The School For Scandal at the National. Her other credits
include *An Evening With Queen Victoria* (1980),
Quartermain's Terms (1981) and *When We Are Married* (1986). She
is pictured here with her husband, actor Timothy West,
whose stage career began in 1956. He has played Prospero, Falstaff
and Shylock, and made rather a speciality of famous
historical figures, including Dr Johnson, Stalin, Churchill and
Jefferson. He also appeared in *Big In Brazil* (1984) and
When We Are Married (1986).

MICHAEL CRAWFORD

Michael Crawford is an actor of immense versatility –
audiences will remember his circus stunts in *Barnum* and the
vibrant voice behind the mask in *The Phantom Of The Opera*.
His big breakthrough came in the long-running
No Sex Please – We're British (1971).

MICHAEL FRAYN

Michael Frayn, who is a novelist as well as an adapter and translator of Russian plays, has written a string of West End hits, including *Donkey's Years* (Globe, 1976), *Make Or Break* (Haymarket, 1980), *Benefactors* (Vaudeville, 1984), the farce *Noises Off* (1982), which ran for four years at the Savoy, and *Look Look* (1990).

JONATHAN PRYCE

Jonathan Pryce made his name in Trevor Griffiths'
Comedians (1975). His other outstanding stage roles
have been in Shakespeare (*Hamlet* at the Royal Court in 1980,
Macbeth at the RSC in 1986), Chekhov (*The Seagull* at the
Queens in 1985, *Uncle Vanya* at the Vaudeville in 1988) and
Miss Saigon (Drury Lane, 1989).

FIONA SHAW

Fiona Shaw's powerful performances in *The Taming Of The Shrew* and *Electra* at the RSC, and as the double lead in *The Good Person Of Sichuan* at the National, have put her in the front rank of Britain's young actresses.

GWEN FRANGCON-DAVIS

Gwen Frangcon-Davis, born in 1896, is one of the legends of the British stage,
having played almost every great role with every great name over seven decades.
Her interpretations of O'Neill (Mary Tyrone in *Long Day's Journey Into Night*, 1958)
and Tennessee Williams (Amanda Wingfield in *The Glass Menagerie*, 1965) were
particularly fine. She still runs actors' workshops.

MICHAEL BRYANT

Michael Bryant has been a National Theatre player since 1977,
often stealing the limelight in roles such as
Enobarbus and Polonius. His first success was as the tutor
in Peter Shaffer's *Five Finger Exercise* (1958).

NATASHA RICHARDSON

Natasha Richardson, continuing the Redgrave family
tradition, played Ophelia at the Young Vic in 1985, Nina
(opposite her mother Vanessa Redgrave) in *The Seagull*, and
Tracy in the Cole Porter musical *High Society*.

DINSDALE LANDEN

Dinsdale Landen has appeared in a multitude of roles since his début on the London Stage in 1957. He has had notable successes in Shaw (*Arms And The Man*, *The Philanderer*), Shakespeare (*The Taming Of The Shrew*, *Twelfth Night*) and Chekhov (*Uncle Vanya*), and a parallel career in farce.

DAVY CUNNINGHAM

Davy Cunningham is a lighting designer, equally at home in
opera and theatre, and much in demand in Britain and abroad.
He designed the lighting for *The Mikado* (ENO), *The Taming
Of The Shrew* (RSC), *A Streetcar Named Desire* (Sheffield)
and *The Possessed* (Almeida).

DEBORAH WARNER

Deborah Warner formed the Kick Theatre Company in 1980,
directing Shakespeare and Brecht. Her productions of *Titus
Andronicus* and *Electra* at the Barbican, and *The Good Person
Of Sichuan* at the National, were highly acclaimed.

PETER SHAFFER

Peter Shaffer is a playwright who has always gone for grand themes vividly expressed – *The Royal Hunt Of The Sun, Equus, Amadeus. Lettuce and Lovage* (1987) explores another favorite theme, the clash between outsider and social conformist.

DEREK JACOBI

Derek Jacobi emerged from the National Youth Theatre to become one of the stars of Olivier's National Theatre. His recent successes have included Richard II and Richard III (played in tandem) at the Phoenix, *Cyrano De Bergerac* at the RSC, and *Hamlet* (also at the Phoenix), in which he directed Kenneth Branagh. Other recent credits include *Breaking The Code* at the Haymarket and *Much Ado About Nothing* at the RSC.

ELAINE PAIGE

Elaine Paige rose to fame in the title role of Andrew Lloyd Webber's *Evita*. She also made a hit in the phenomenally successful *Cats*, *Chess*, and the Cole Porter revival *Anything Goes*.

MARGARET 'PERCY' HARRIS

Margaret 'Percy' Harris was part of a three-woman group called Motley (with Audrey Harris and Elizabeth Montgomery) that began designing for the Old Vic in 1932, presenting many of John Gielgud's productions (*Richard II, The School For Scandal, The Merchant Of Venice, The Importance Of Being Earnest*). Motley continued until the 1970s.

ALEX JENNINGS

Alex Jennings, in *Ghetto* at the National, *The Liar* at the
Old Vic, *The Wild Duck* at the Phoenix, *The Taming Of The
Shrew* at the RSC, and Ostrovsky's *Too Clever By Half*, again
at the Old Vic, has proved himself to be one of Britain's
most exciting young actors.

SIMON CALLOW

Simon Callow created the role of Mozart in Peter Shaffer's *Amadeus* at the National Theatre. His vast range of parts has included Orlando in *As You Like It* at the National and *Faust* at the Lyric, Hammersmith. He also appeared in Alan Bennett's double bill *Single Spies* at the National, directing the second part. He also directs opera.

LINDSAY DUNCAN

Lindsay Duncan played the amoral Marquise de Merteuil
in the RSC's hugely successful adaptation of Laclos'
Les Liaisons Dangereuses (1986) in London and on
Broadway. She then triumphed as Hedda Gabler at the Hampstead
Theatre, and as Maggie in *Cat On A Hot Tin Roof* and in
Berenice at the National.

HAROLD PINTER

Harold Pinter's first full-length play, *The Birthday Party* (1958), was met with wide incomprehension. Since then *The Caretaker*, *The Homecoming*, *No Man's Land* and *Betrayal* have established him as one of Britain's most distinguished dramatists.

SIR JOHN MILLS

Sir John Mills has alternated between stage and screen throughout his distinguished 60-year career. Starting in revue in the 1930s, he moved into straight plays and into 'uniform' films. In recent years he has appeared in *Ross*, *Veterans*, *Little Lies* and *Dandy Dick*.

HARRIET WALTER

Harriet Walter began her stage career with the agit-prop group 7.84, but her Ophelia at the Royal Court in 1980 signalled a change of direction. Since then she has been seen at the RSC, as Helena in *All's Well That Ends Well*, in *Henry IV – Parts I and II*, as Viola in *Twelfth Night*, Masha in *The Three Sisters* and the Duchess of Malfi.

NABIL SHABAN

Nabil Shaban has been acclaimed for his performances in *Iranian Nights* and as Haile Selassie in *The Emperor*. He also works in radio and TV (*Walter*). His energies helped to found the GRAEAE theatre group for disabled performers.

RICHARD EYRE

Richard Eyre, formerly with the Royal Lyceum in Edinburgh
and the Nottingham Playhouse, became Artistic Director of
the National Theatre in 1988. *Guys And Dolls, Bartholemew
Fair, Hamlet, Schweyk In The Second World War,
The Government Inspector, The Beggar's Opera* and
The Changeling have been among his most successful productions
on the South Bank.

Directors are – or should be – invisible creatures who emerge only rarely, like moles, into the light. None of the directors in this book would subscribe to the notion of Directors' Theatre, not because, God forbid, they're without vanity, but because they know the theatre to be a collaborative art. A director who didn't recognise the supremacy of the actor would not only be fatally vain but also very foolish.

A director needs to be somehow assertive and yet self-effacing, dogged and yet pliable, demanding yet supportive. If this sounds like a prescription for a perfect marriage partner, then I suppose it is. These photographs are a gallery of prospective professional spouses ever hopeful of making a successful marriage of actor and director, text and design, play and audience. If they look a hesitant, doubtful, diffident lot it is because they know just how difficult it is, as in real life, to make a marriage work.

RICHARD EYRE

JANE LAPOTAIRE

Jane Lapotaire has a special gift for playing tragic
heroines – Edith Piaf, Joan of Arc, Antigone, and most
recently the dying wife of C. S. Lewis in *Shadowlands*.
She has also appeared in *Double Double* at the Fortune and in
Greenland at the Royal Court.

ANDREW LLOYD WEBBER

Andrew Lloyd Webber is a producer – he heads the Really Useful Company, which put on *Daisy Pulls It Off* at the Globe in 1983, *On Your Toes* at the Palace in 1984 and *Aspects Of Love* at the Prince of Wales in 1989 – as well as the most successful composer of British musicals ever. *Jesus Christ Superstar*, *Evita*, *Cats*, *Starlight Express*, *The Phantom Of The Opera* and *Aspects Of Love* have all had extended runs.

ANTHONY SHER

Anthony Sher has appeared in the West End, at the National Theatre and, most memorably, at the RSC as Shylock, the Fool in *King Lear*, and Richard III. His other RSC credits include *Molière* (1983), *Tartuffe* (1984) and *Singer* (1989).

NICOLA PAGETT

Nicola Pagett has appeared in many all-star casts in plays
such as *Voyage Round My Father* (Haymarket, 1971),
Ayckbourn's *Taking Steps* (Lyric, 1980), *The Trojan War Will
Not Take Place* (National, 1982), *The School For Scandal*
(Duke of York, 1984), and *Aren't We All?* and *Old Times*
(Haymarket, 1984 and 1985).

STEFANOS LAZARIDIS

Stefanos Lazaridis, Associate Designer at the ENO, has designed more than 20 productions, including *Tosca* (set in Mussolini's Italy), *Hansel And Gretel*, and *The Mikado* (set in 1920s England). He has also designed for leading opera houses in Florence, Stuttgart, Berlin, San Francisco, Nice and Bologna.

DAVID SUCHET

David Suchet's performances on TV, especially as Sigmund
Freud and Hercule Poirot, have gained him a very wide
public. During his 12 years at the RSC he played Iago,
Shylock and Lear's Fool, and in *Once In A Lifetime*. He
appeared in *Separation* at the Comedy in 1988.

JULIA MCKENZIE

Julia McKenzie made her mark in Ayckbourn (*The Norman Conquests, Ten Times Table, Woman In Mind*) and Brecht (*Schweyk In The Second World War*) and has sung in musicals such as *Company, Follies, Side By Side By Sondheim, Promises Promises* and *Guys And Dolls* at the National.

SUSAN HAMPSHIRE

Susan Hampshire has appeared in a wide variety of plays,
including *Night And Day*, *Peter Pan*, *Taming Of The Shrew*,
A Doll's House, *Man And Superman*, *As You Like It*,
Blithe Spirit, *Married Love* and *A Little Night Music*.
She is seen here with her husband, Eddie Kulukundis,
impresario and publisher.

TREVOR NUNN

Trevor Nunn ran the RSC from 1968 to 1986, directing
productions such as *The Relapse*, *The Comedy of Errors*,
The Alchemist, *Juno And The Paycock*, *Nicholas Nickleby* and
Les Misérables. *Cats* and *Starlight Express*, both huge West End
and worldwide hits, were also directed by him.

JANET SUZMAN

Janet Suzman made her reputation at the RSC, then went on to play Hedda Gabler, Masha in *The Three Sisters* (Cambridge), Andromache (Old Vic), and in *Another Time* (Wyndhams). In 1989 she directed *Othello* in her native South Africa.

NICHOLAS HYTNER

Nicholas Hytner directed many memorable opera productions
at the Coliseum and Covent Garden before luring actor
John Wood back to the British stage for *The Tempest* and
King Lear at the Old Vic. His most recent successes have been
Ghetto and *Miss Saigon*.

DESMOND BARRITT

Desmond Barritt is a fine comic actor. He has portrayed Feste in *Twelfth Night* at the RSC, Banjo in *The Man Who Came To Dinner*, and most recently a hilarious valet in *The Liar* at the Old Vic.

IMOGEN STUBBS

Imogen Stubbs, a graduate of Oxford University, RADA and rep, played opposite Jeremy Irons in the RSC's *Richard II* and *The Rover* (1986–87), and in *The Two Noble Kinsman* (RSC, 1987). She has also appeared in numerous films and TV plays.

STEPHEN PIMLOTT

Stephen Pimlott made his name directing opera at the ENO,
Opera North and Covent Garden, and *Carmen* at Earl's Court.
After two years of theatre at Sheffield, he returned to
music, directing Sondheim's *Sunday In The Park With George*
at the National (1990).

DANGER
Overhead
hazard

TOM STOPPARD

Tom Stoppard had his first taste of success with *Rosencrantz and Guildenstern Are Dead* in 1966. Since then he has written *Jumpers, Dirty Linen, Travesties, Night And Day, The Real Thing* and *Hapgood*, all full of verbal wit, literary jokes and intellectual games.

PATRICIA ROUTLEDGE

Patricia Routledge is a comedienne, a fine soprano – as she
has proved in a number of musicals in London and on Broadway –
and also a dramatic actress (*Noises Off, When We Are
Married, Richard III, Candide*). TV audiences will remember
her in plays by Alan Bennett.

PETER BOWLES

Peter Bowles' stage career has included roles in Tom
Stoppard (*Dirty Linen*) and Alan Ayckbourn (*Absent Friends,
Man Of The Moment*). His other credits include *Born In The
Gardens* (Globe, 1980), *The Entertainer* (Shaftesbury, 1986)
and *Canaries Sometimes Sing* (Albery, 1987).

DAME JUDI DENCH

Dame Judi Dench, now a director as well as a performer,
first stepped into the limelight at the Old Vic in 1960 as a
radiant Juliet. Since then she has triumphed in many other
Shakespearean roles, in Pinter and Brecht, in films,
and on TV. Her recent stage appearances have included
Mr and Mrs Nobody at the Garrick, and *Entertaining Strangers* and
Hamlet at the National.

There is so much written about the glamour and excitement of an actor's life that one is sometimes tempted to say it isn't really like that at all. That, far from enjoying late mornings and even later nights, most actors spend their free time tending to the housework, seeing their accountants, agents, doctors and dentists, taking children to school, picking children up from school, doing the shopping, and so on. If they are in the theatre, they will find their way to a cramped dressing room – usually up or down several flights of stairs – put on a costume and make–up, and for a few hours become Othello, Juliet,

Horatio, Third Witch, Soldier. . . . Or it may be endless hours of coffee in plastic cups and dog-eared sandwiches while recording a television or radio play. Or a long night freezing in a muddy field fighting the Battle of Agincourt.

The hours are often long, the appearances sometimes painfully brief, the audiences small. But none of that really matters. The heart of *our* mystery is a tremendous need to communicate, to tell a story, to share knowledge, tears, laughter.

Come to think of it, what could be more glamorous, or more exciting!

JUDI DENCH

BOB HOSKINS

Bob Hoskins has played many parts in rep and at the Royal Court, and seasons at the RSC and National Theatre (*True West*, *Guys And Dolls*). His other credits include *Pygmalion*, *Has Washington Legs* and *The World Turned Upside Down*. On TV he has played Iago and in *Pennies From Heaven*.

ZOË WANAMAKER

Zoë Wanamaker, daughter of actor Sam Wanamaker, established herself at the RSC in *Once In A Lifetime*, *The Comedy Of Errors*, *Twelfth Night* (Viola) and *Mrs Klein*. She also played Gwendolen in the National's *The Importance Of Being Earnest*.

NIGEL HAWTHORNE

Nigel Hawthorne established his reputation at the Royal
Court in *Early Morning* (1968) and *West Of Suez* (1971). His
greatest successes have been in *Privates on Parade* and *Tartuffe* at the
RSC, *The Magistrate* at the National, and most recently in
Shadowlands and Tom Stoppard's *Hapgood*.

ALAN AYCKBOURN

Alan Ayckbourn has written a string of hits since *Relatively Speaking* reached the London stage in 1967 – *How The Other Half Loves*, *Absurd Person Singular*, *The Norman Conquests*, *A Chorus Of Disapproval*, *Henceforward* and *Man Of The Moment*. He has also directed for the National Theatre (*A Small Family Business* in 1987 and *View From The Bridge* in 1988).

RUDOLPH WALKER

Rudolph Walker has appeared in *Gloo Joo, Sitwe Banzi Is Dead* and *Playboy Of The West Indies,* and in the TV series *Black Silk.* He has also played Caliban in two productions of *The Tempest* by Jonathan Miller.

DOROTHY TUTIN

Dorothy Tutin joined the RSC at the age of 20, returning
many years later as Shakespeare's Cleopatra. Her remarkable
range has encompassed Madame Ranevsky in *The Cherry Orchard*,
Lady Macbeth, the Jewish mother in Neil Simon's *Brighton
Beach Memoirs*, and Restoration comedy.

PETER GILL

Peter Gill began his theatrical career as an actor, then became a director at the Royal Court, the Riverside and the National Theatre. He is also a playwright – his best known play, *Mean Tears*, is about a painful love affair.

DAVID MORRISSEY

David Morrissey appeared in the Cheek By Jowl Company's
El Cid and *Twelfth Night*, then in *King John* and *Richard III*
at the RSC. Most recently he has appeared at the National
in *Ghetto* and as the younger *Peer Gynt* (1990).

WILLY RUSSELL

Willy Russell is a song-writer, singer and dramatist. His first stage hit was *John, Paul, George, Ringo And . . . Bert* in 1978. This was followed by *Educating Rita*, *Blood Brothers* and *Shirley Valentine*, nominated for two Oscars.

CAMERON MACKINTOSH

Cameron Mackintosh has produced plays and musicals – nearly 200 so far – all over the world. His greatest successes have been *Les Misérables, Cats, Little Shop Of Horrors, Side By Side By Sondheim, The Phantom Of The Opera, Aspects Of Love, Trelawney, Song And Dance, Anything Goes, Follies* and *Miss Saigon*.

PENELOPE KEITH

Penelope Keith made her London début in 1964, then
established herself as an exponent of high comedy in plays
by Shaw (*The Millionairess, Captain Brassbound's Conversion,
The Apple Cart*), Coward (*Hay Fever*) and Ayckbourn
(*The Norman Conquests*). She has recently appeared in
The Merry Wives Of Windsor at Chichester.

JOHN MORTIMER

John Mortimer wrote his first play, *Dock Brief*, in 1957.
This drew on his experiences as a barrister, as did his
highly popular TV series *Rumpole Of The Bailey*. His biggest
stage successes have been *A Voyage Round My Father* and
translations of Feydeau farces (*A Little Hotel On The Side*,
A Flea In Her Ear).

Play writing is an extremely worrying business. Perhaps this accounts for the look of anxiety on the faces of many playwrights. Writing the work is the easiest part. You may get cold, you may be lonely, but a play, compared to a novel, is a relatively short stint and could be completed, Noel Coward boasted, in a weekend. But when it's written the troubles begin. You have an ideal actor or actress but they're busy, or want to spend more time with their family, or just don't want to go out at night. After nine months waiting you settle for the ninth choice. If you've found a director he wants changes, or makes impossible demands – 'Just one brilliantly funny line, please, for the middle of Scene Two.' Is there going to be a theatre available? What about the play at the 'Proscenium'? You hear business is shaky there and go along hopefully, but the 'Proscenium' is found to be full of cheering, laughing people. Finally you settle for the old 'Curtain' theatre down a side street with no passing trade. If you survive the notices by the skin of your teeth there follows a long period of taking the play's temperature with the help of the weekly returns. Is business down because it's Holy Week, or raining, or too hot, or simply because no one likes it very much and your work is about to enter the limbo of forgotten plays?

But, and it's a big but, when it's good the theatre is more rewarding than anything else for a writer. It's rewarding because, if he can only hold his customers' attention and stop them rustling chocolate papers or dying of bronchitis, they will do anything for him. If he puts a chair on an empty stage and says it's a throne room, they will believe him. If he tells them a living actor's a ghost, they will also believe him. In the theatre the writer and the audience collaborate in an act of imagination which is a play in perform-ance. And when they all laugh together, with a single voice, there is nothing quite like it. So that may account for the look of cheerfulness on the faces of some of the playwrights in this book.   JOHN MORTIMER

NED SHERRIN

Ned Sherrin is a film and TV producer, writer, and media
personality as well as a theatre director. In the latter
role his achievements have included *Side By Side By Sondheim*
(in which he also appeared), *Mr And Mrs Nobody* and
Jeffrey Bernard Is Unwell.

JANE ASHER

Jane Asher began her acting career in Shakespeare (Juliet, Perdita) and now divides her time between stage and TV. She was a great success in Ayckbourn's *Henceforward* (1989), in which she played the robot. She is seen here with her husband, Gerald Scarfe, cartoonist and stage designer (*Orpheus In The Underworld*, ENO, 1985).

TOM CONTI

Tom Conti made his West End début in *Savages* (1973), then triumphed in London and on Broadway in *Whose Life Is It Anyway?* Other performances, between films, have included *They're Playing Our Song*, *Romantic Comedy*, *An Italian Straw Hat* and the title role in *Jeffrey Bernard Is Unwell*.

ALAN BENNETT

Alan Bennett is an actor, director and playwright. His most successful stage plays have included *Habeas Corpus* (1973) and *The Old Country* (1977), and *Forty Years On* (1968) and *Single Spies* (1988), in which he also acted. He also directed *An Englishman Abroad*, the first part of *Single Spies* at the National. TV audiences know him best as the chronicler of 'quietly desperate' northern lives.

RONALD HARWOOD

Ronald Harwood's most successful play, *The Dresser* (1980),
was based on his experiences as an actor and dresser in Sir Donald
Wolfit's company. *Another Time* (1989) was also a
semi-autobiographical piece.

ATHENE SEYLER

Athene Seyler, born in 1889, made her first stage appearance
at the beginning of this century. She excelled in comedies,
particularly those of Shakespeare, Sheridan, Wilde, Shaw and
Pinero. Her most famous roles were Miss Prism and Lady
Bracknell in *The Importance Of Being Earnest*, Lady Fidget in
The Country Wife, Mrs Candour in *The School For Scandal*, the
nurse in *Romeo And Juliet*, and Mrs Malaprop in *The Rivals*.

GRIFF RHYS JONES

Griff Rhys Jones, fresh from the Cambridge Footlights, became a celebrity as part of the *Not The Nine O'Clock News* team. In between his many TV appearances he has starred in *Charley's Aunt*, Dario Fo's *Trumpets And Raspberries* and in Ben Travers' *Thark*.

STEVEN BERKOFF

Steven Berkoff formed the London Theatre Group in 1968,
directing adaptations of Kafka (*The Trial*), Aeschylus
(*Agamemnon*) and Poe (*The Fall Of The House Of Usher*). His
original stage plays, in which he has also acted, include
East, *Greek*, *Harry's Christmas*, *Lunch*, *West*, *Acapulco*,
Sink The Belgrano! and *Massage*. In 1989 he took his Edinburgh
Festival production of Wilde's *Salome* to the National.

ELIJAH MOSHINSKY

Elijah Moshinsky directed opera at Covent Garden and the ENO
before turning his talents to straight plays. His most
recent successes include *The Three Sisters*, *Another Time* and
Shadowlands. He has also directed Shakespeare for TV.

MARGARET TYZACK

Margaret Tyzack, who made her London début in 1959, recently appeared in London and on Broadway in *Lettuce and Lovage*. Her performances in *Who's Afraid Of Virginia Woolf?*, *All's Well That Ends Well* and *Tom And Viv* received special acclaim.

DECLAN DONNELLAN

Declan Donnellan (left) founded the Cheek By Jowl touring theatre
company in 1981, a small ensemble doing plays with great
economy of means. Under his direction the company has given
inspired reinterpretations of many classics. In 1990 he
directed *Peer Gynt* at the National. He is seen here with Nick
Ormerod, co-founder and joint artistic director of the company.

MAX STAFFORD-CLARK

Max Stafford-Clark has run the Royal Court Theatre since 1981, directing such productions as *Tom And Viv*, *Our Country's Good*, *Borderline*, *Bent*, *Road*, *The Normal Heart* and *The Recruiting Officer*, and plays by Caryl Churchill (*Cloud 9*, *Top Girls*, *Serious Money*).

EILEEN ATKINS

Eileen Atkins has played many formidable women in the past
20 years – Medea, Virginia Woolf in *A Room Of One's Own*,
Elizabeth I (*Vivat! Vivat Regina!*), Hedda Gabler, Electra,
the Duchess of Malfi, and Shaw's Saint Joan.

WILLIAM GASKILL

William Gaskill has been Associate Director of the National Theatre (1963–65) and Director of the Royal Court (1965–75), and has recently renewed his association with the National by directing Pirandello's *Man, Beast And Virtue* (1989). In the early '80s he directed *She Stoops To Conquer*, *The Relapse* and *Rents* at the Lyric Hammersmith, and *The Way Of The World* at the Haymarket.

JOHN GUNTER

John Gunter's designs have enriched many productions –
Guys And Dolls, *Wild Honey*, *High Society*, *The Government
Inspector*, *The Secret Rapture*. He has designed for the
Royal Court, Chichester, the RSC, the National, and in
Europe and on Broadway.

DUNCAN WELDON

Duncan Weldon has produced more than 125 plays in the West
End, the most recent (with Jerome Minskoff) being *Long Day's
Journey Into Night* with Jack Lemmon and Sir Peter Hall's
Orpheus Descending and *The Merchant of Venice*.

MONA HAMMOND

Mona Hammond went from RADA to the Young Vic in
The Crucible, then appeared in *The Great White Hope* at the
RSC and as Åse in the National's *Peer Gynt* (1990). She has
also appeared in *Eastenders* and other TV series.

CARL TOMS

There is a lot of flip and flashy comment in the media about Directors' Theatre, Actors' Theatre and Designers' Theatre. This, I'm afraid, is rubbishy politics invented by a desperate and over-zealous press who daily need to fill up their newspapers, magazines and chat shows. There is only one theatre: that which entertains, disturbs and excites.

The designer makes a very powerful contribution to all of these things. Everyone with half an eye responds to visual stimulus, and when that stimulus is in tune with the written text, then something approaching theatrical excitement will occur. The chemistry is delicate and calls for a concentrated collaboration with the director and actors and lighting designer.

Design in the theatre is a frequently misunderstood art, or craft. It earned a bad reputation in its early years as being the province of dilettanti, and the public still has the romantically misleading idea that designers sit down one sunny afternoon and do a pretty sketch and pass it wanly on to a clever technician before drifting off to yet another cocktail party. Nothing could be further from the truth. Theatrical design is seeringly hard work, shattering to the nerves, involving endless meetings, ferocious arguments with directors and producers, battles with actors, tussles over budgets . . . and if you don't get careful or clever you are rendered down into a compliant puddle. The art is thrown out with the bath water.

There has been an exciting decentralisation of theatre in Britain. Major centres of theatrical originality once confined to just a few cities have now expanded to all corners of these islands, bringing many opportunities for young designers to stretch their wings, which they have done, coping with all the financial limitations. There can be a direct relationship between financial economy and artistic economy. One can foster the other, in clever hands. There is always more there than you need.

Of course, the great subsidised theatres give great opportunities. It is blissful to have the financial and technical backing of a major theatrical organisation, and we have quite a few – although fewer than we should have compared with the continent of Europe – capable of giving us dazzling productions, brilliantly designed and very exciting. In recent years there has been a tendency towards the European school of design. Effective as it is, it isn't always deeply caring of the text, which frequently gets mangled. In the drift towards originality, the text can, and often does, end up as window dressing.

All the same, over the last three decades we have had important foreign influences. Joseph Stoboda, for example, broke through our natural tendency to realism and used projections and quirky materials with great inventive sucess. Nearer home, Peter Brook, having started by doing highly decorative and romantic productions such as *Ring Round The Moon* using Oliver Messel as his designer, slowly evolved into the great theatrical guru that he is today, making design inseparable from the director's conception.

It might be said that now the two *are* inseparable. A great production is usually seamless. The collaboration is complicated, laborious, and often agonising and tempestuous, but it is the essential process through which a piece of design must go if it is to be any good.

We have a dazzling school of theatrical design in this country. From the extravagant excesses of the state-subsidised companies to the careful, bold economy of Cheek by Jowl, who know which images will remain with us?

CARL TOMS

Carl Toms, the first Head of Design at the Young Vic, has
designed many Tom Stoppard plays (*Jumpers*, *The Real Thing*,
Hapgood), Anthony Shaffer's *Sleuth*, and Michael Frayn's
Look Look. He also redesigned the Theatre Royal in Bath and
restored London's Cambridge and Garrick theatres.

MARIA FRIEDMAN

Maria Friedman has sung in musicals at the Bristol Old Vic,
Cavalcade at Chichester, *Blondel* and *Blues In The Night* in
the West End, and in *Ghetto* and *Sunday In The Park With
George* at the National.

TIM RICE

Tim Rice wrote the lyrics for *Joseph And The Amazing Technicolor Dreamcoat*, *Jesus Christ Superstar*, *Evita*, *Blondel*, *Chess* and *Starmania*. He is also a publisher and broadcaster.

TONY HARRISON

Tony Harrison – linguist, classicist and poet – was responsible for transplanting Molière's *Misanthrope* to the Paris of 1968 and Racine's *Phèdre* to colonial India, and for writing *The Mysteries* in Yorkshire dialect. *The Trackers Of Oxyrynchus* (1990) was built upon a fragment by Sophocles.

MARIA AITKIN

Maria Aitkin entered the theatre via OUDS, and has
been mainly associated with the plays of Noel Coward
(*Private Lives, Design For Living, Blithe Spirit,
The Vortex*). She also directs.

DONALD SINDEN

Donald Sinden has moved, with great success, between classical theatre (*The Relapse, London Assurance, The School For Scandal, King Lear, Othello*), West End comedy (*There's A Girl In My Soup, Two Into One*), and TV situation comedy (*Never The Twain*).

SIR PETER HALL

Sir Peter Hall ran the RSC from 1960 to 1968, and the National Theatre from 1973 to 1988 (*Hamlet*, *No Man's Land*, *Amadeus*, *The Oresteia*, *Coriolanus*). He then formed his own company, directing *Orpheus Descending* (with Vanessa Redgrave), *The Merchant of Venice* (with Dustin Hoffman) and *The Wild Duck*.

JOCELYN HERBERT

Jocelyn Herbert studied theatre design under George Devine, director of the Royal Court, and did most of her early work there (the Wesker Trilogy, *Sergeant Musgrave's Dance*, *A Patriot For Me*). Since then she has designed hundreds of plays, operas and films all over the world. For the National she designed *Othello*, *Mother Courage* and *Galileo*, and for the RSC *Ghosts* and *Richard III*.

KENNETH BRANAGH

Kenneth Branagh went directly from RADA into *Another Country* in the West End. After working with the RSC, he formed the Renaissance Theatre Company, for which he played Hamlet. He directed and starred in the acclaimed film of *Henry V*.

DANIEL DAY LEWIS

Daniel Day Lewis began his career at the Bristol Old Vic. He then appeared in *Romeo And Juliet* (RSC tour), *The Futurists* (National), and on Shaftsbury Avenue in *Another Country*. He played Hamlet at the National in 1989, as pictured here.

ROBERT STEPHENS

Robert Stephens was one of the stars of Olivier's National Theatre, appearing in *The Recruiting Officer, Much Ado About Nothing* and as the Inca emperor Atahualpa in Shaffer's *The Royal Hunt Of The Sun*. He has since appeared in Chekhov, Ibsen and Shakespeare.

JOHN NAPIER

John Napier, Associate Designer at the RSC, has designed many Shakespeare productions as well as *The Greeks*, *Nicholas Nickleby*, *Mother Courage* and *Peter Pan*. In the commercial theatre he is best known for his settings of *Cats*, *Starlight Express*, *Time* and *Les Misérables*.

CARYL CHURCHILL

Caryl Churchill is a dramatist who tackles topical themes with great verve and invention. *Cloud 9* (1979) and *Top Girls* (1982) were about sexual politics and the award-winning *Serious Money* (1987), which played on Broadway, satirised the City.

SIR MICHAEL HORDERN

Sir Michael Hordern's half century in the theatre has
been dominated by Shakespeare – Polonius, Malvolio,
Prospero, Cassius, King Lear – at Stratford and the Old Vic.
His great gift for comedy has been displayed in many
modern plays and films.

IRVING WARDLE

Irving Wardle was drama critic for *The Times* from 1963 to 1990, and now writes for *The Independent On Sunday*. His play, *The Houseboy*, was performed at the Open Space in 1973.

INDEX